Famous & Fun Deluxe Collection

26 Pieces from Famous & Fun:
Pop, Classics, Favorites, Rock, Duets

Carol Matz

Famous & Fun Deluxe Collection, Book 2, contains 26 well-loved selections drawn from the following books:

- Famous & Fun Pop, Book 2
- Famous & Fun Favorites, Book 2
- Famous & Fun Duets, Book 2
- Famous & Fun Classics, Book 2
- Famous & Fun Rock, Book 2
- Famous & Fun Pop Duets, Book 2

These teacher-tested arrangements are student favorites, and can be used as a supplement to any method. No eighth notes or dotted-quarter rhythms are used. In addition to the wide variety of styles featured in this collection, a few equal-part (primo/secondo) duets are also included for students to have fun with ensemble playing.

Carol Matz

Alfred Music
P.O. Box 10003
Van Nuys, CA 91410-0003
alfred.com

ISBN-10: 0-7390-9867-5
ISBN-13: 978-0-7390-9867-7

(Meet) The Flintstones

Words and Music by
Joseph Barbera, William Hanna and Hoyt Curtin
Arranged by Carol Matz

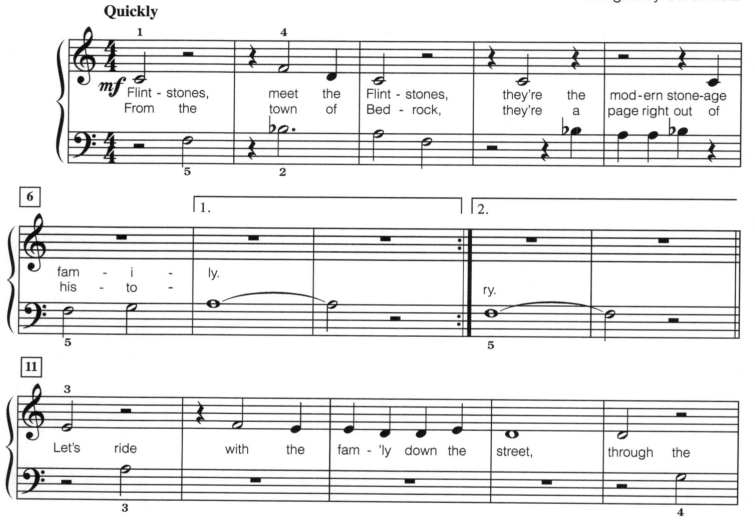

DUET PART (Student plays one octave higher)

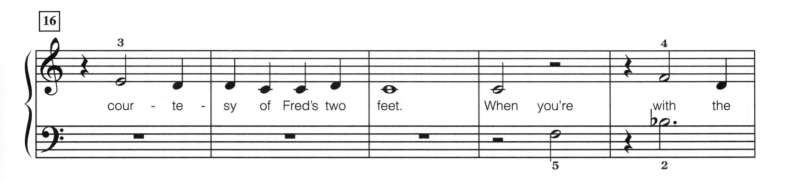

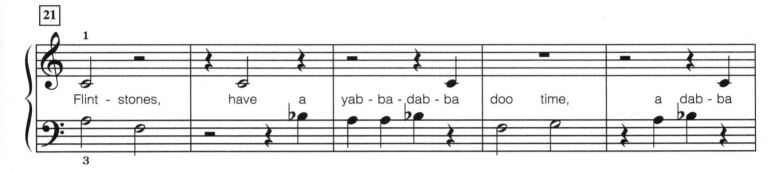

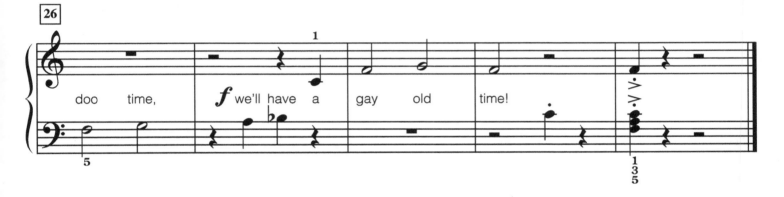

DUET PART (Continued)

4

A Whole New World
(from Walt Disney's "Aladdin")

Words by Tim Rice
Music by Alan Menken
Arranged by Carol Matz

Flowing quickly

A whole new world, a new fan -

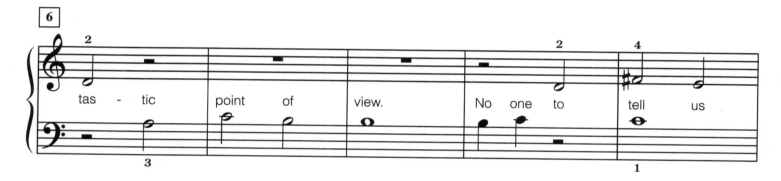

tas - tic point of view. No one to tell us

no or where to go or say we're on - ly dream - ing. A

DUET PART (Student plays one octave higher)

Flowing quickly (in two)

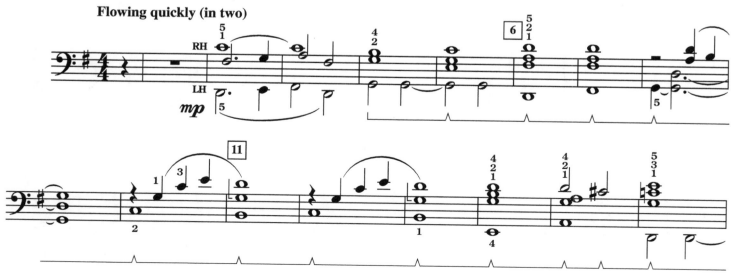

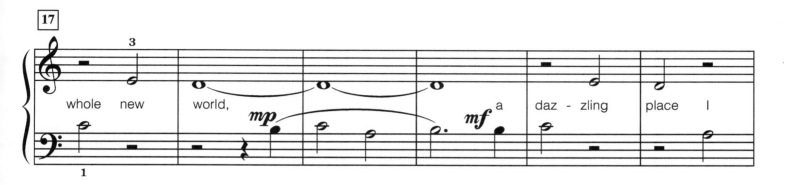

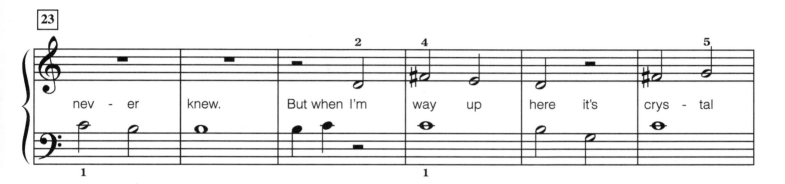

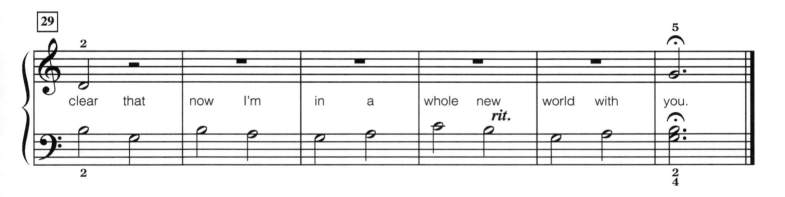

DUET PART (Continued)

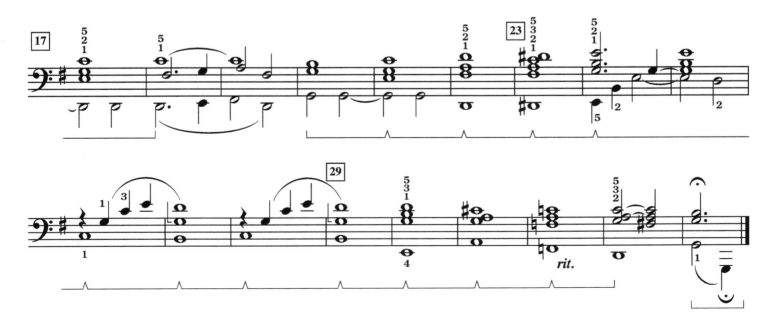

From the Twentieth Century Fox Motion Picture "Star Wars"

Star Wars

(Main Title)

Music by **JOHN WILLIAMS**
Arranged by Carol Matz

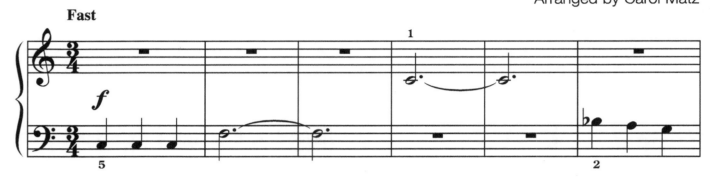

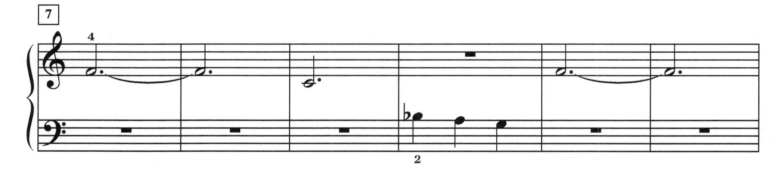

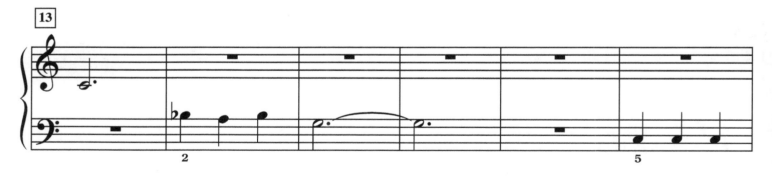

DUET PART (Student plays one octave higher)

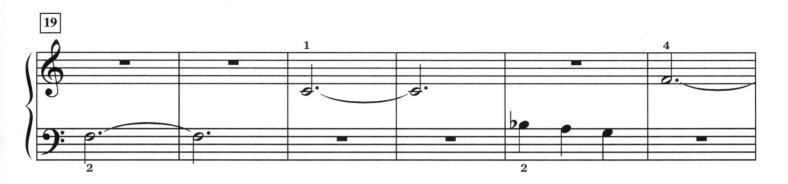

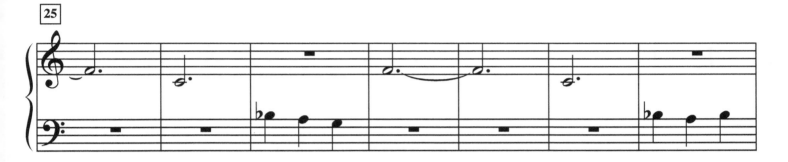

DUET PART (Continued)

Zip-a-Dee-Doo-Dah

(from Walt Disney's "Song of the South")

Words by Ray Gilbert
Music by Allie Wrubel
Arranged by Carol Matz

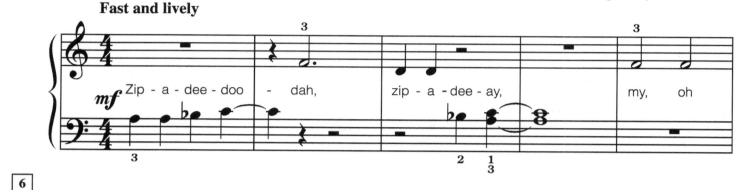

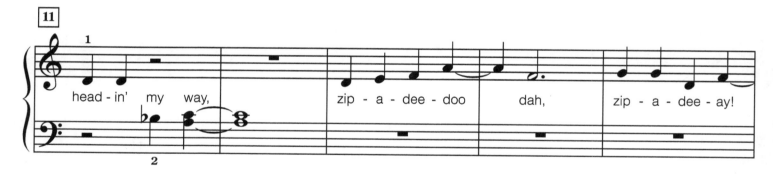

DUET PART (Student plays one octave higher)

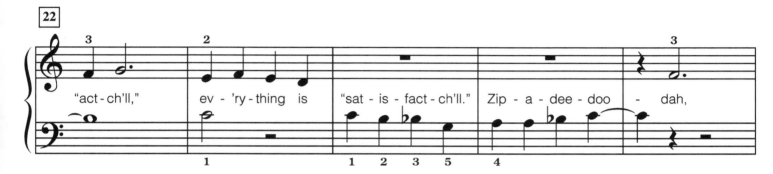

DUET PART (Continued)

James Bond Theme

Music by Monty Norman
Arranged by Carol Matz

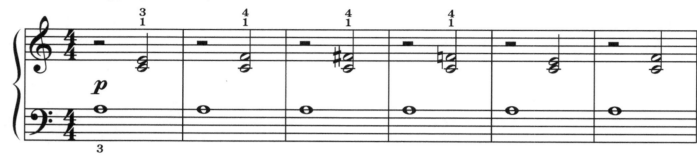

DUET PART (Student plays one octave higher)

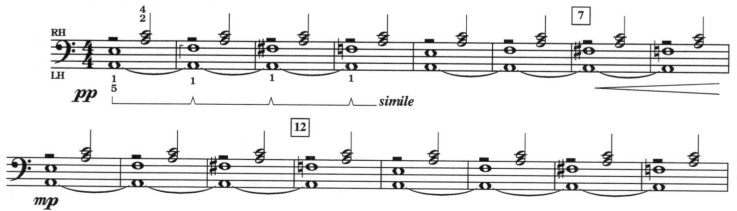

DUET PART (Continued)

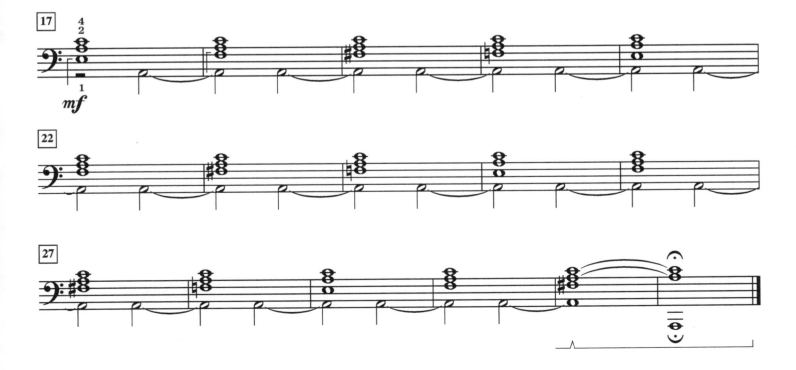

Theme from
Fantasy-Impromptu

Frédéric Chopin (1810–1849)
Arranged by Carol Matz

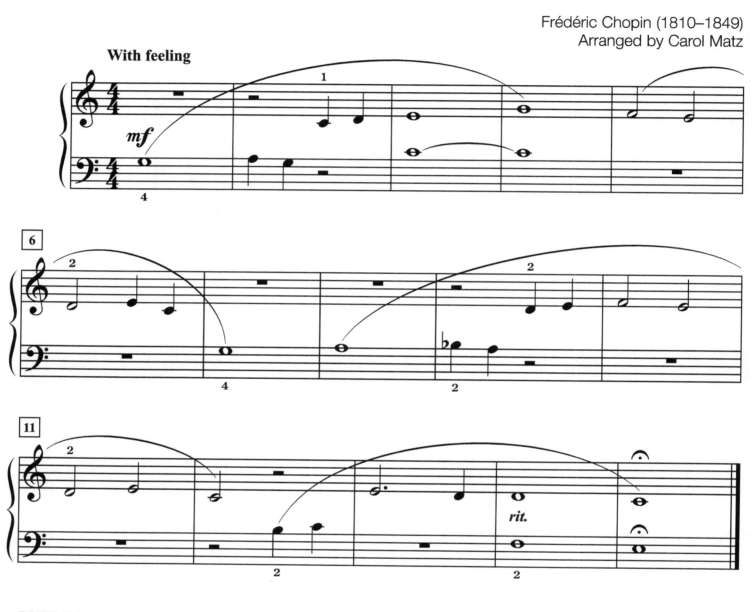

DUET PART (Student plays one octave higher)

Pavane

Gabriel Fauré (1845–1924)
Arranged by Carol Matz

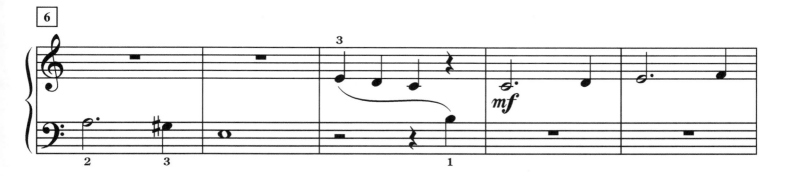

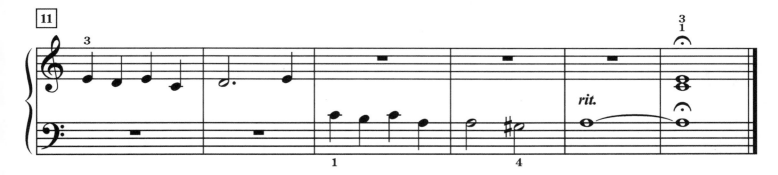

DUET PART (Student plays one octave higher)

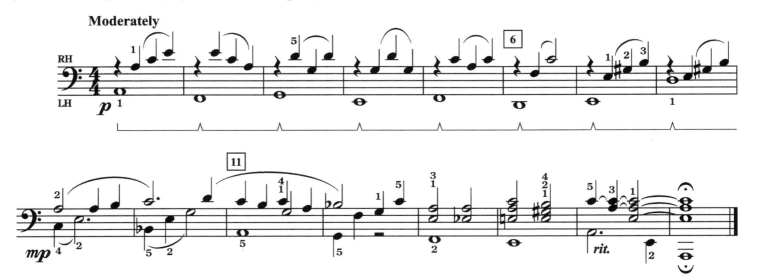

The Merry Widow Waltz

Franz Lehár (1870–1948)
Arranged by Carol Matz

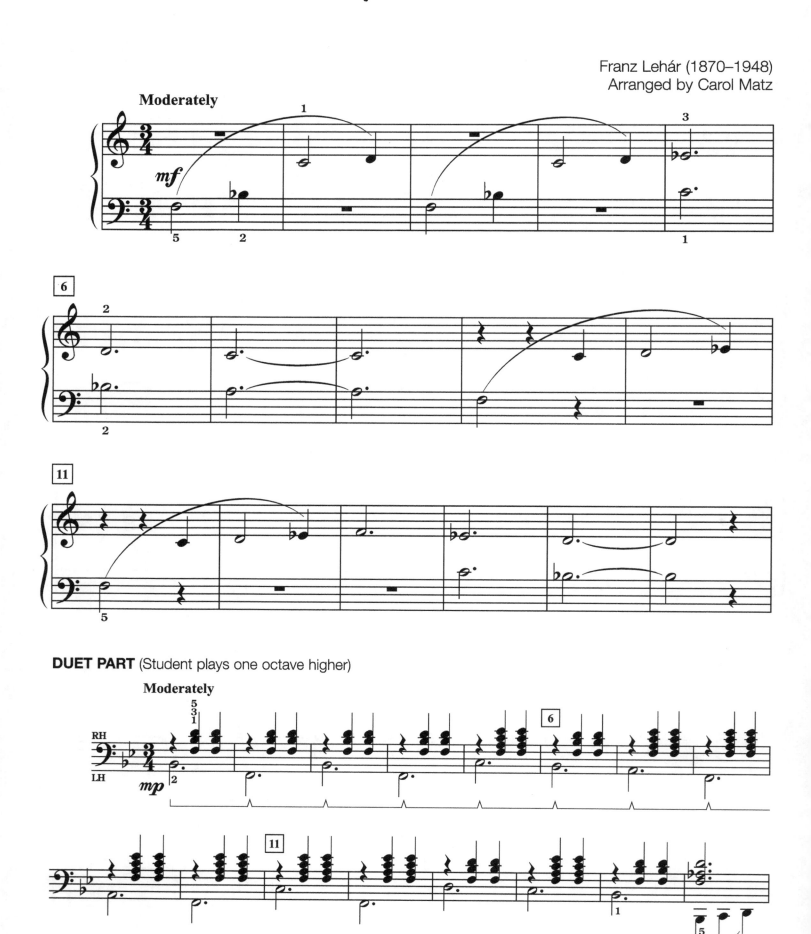

DUET PART (Student plays one octave higher)

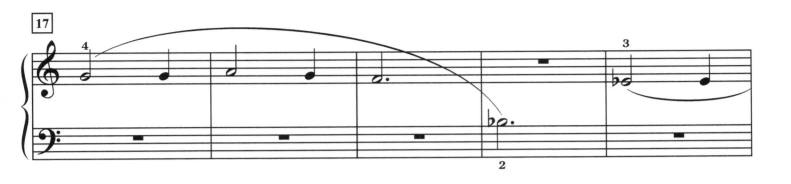

DUET PART (Continued)

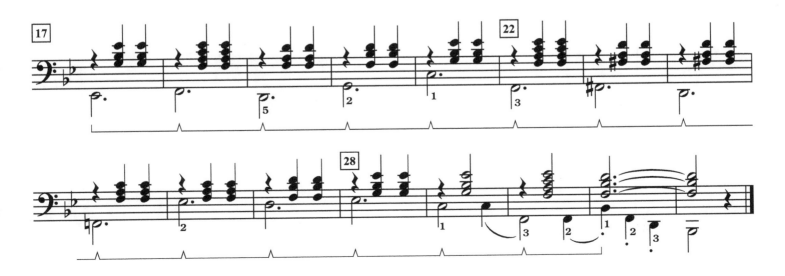

Can-Can

(from the operetta *Orpheus in the Underworld*)

Jacques Offenbach (1819–1880)
Arranged by Carol Matz

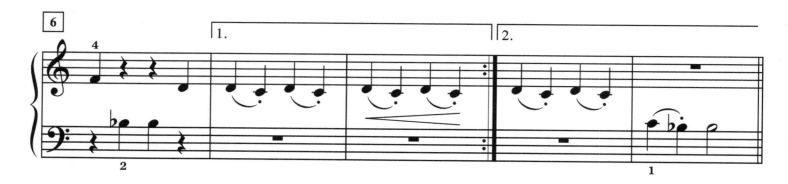

DUET PART (Student plays one octave higher)

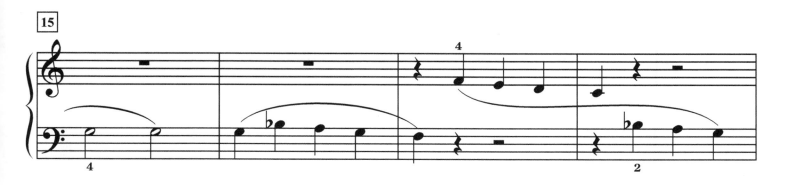

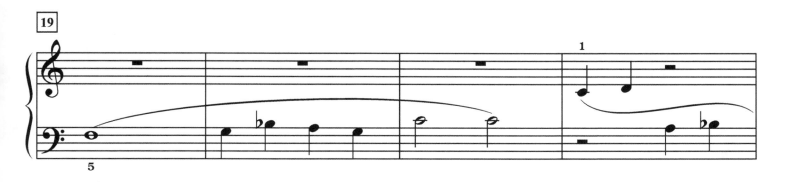

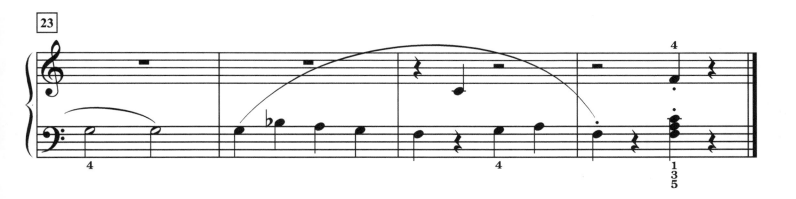

DUET PART (Continued)

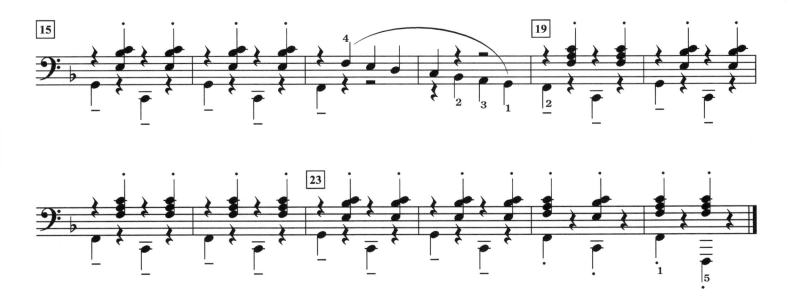

Rondeau

(from *Suite de Symphonies, No. 1*)

Jean-Joseph Mouret (1682–1738)
Arranged by Carol Matz

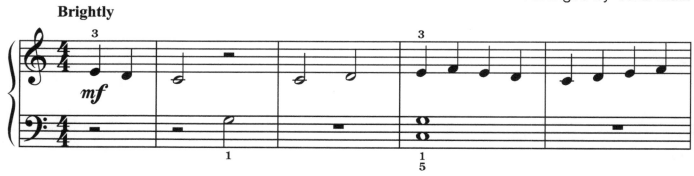

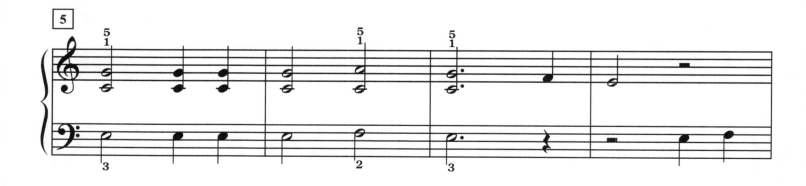

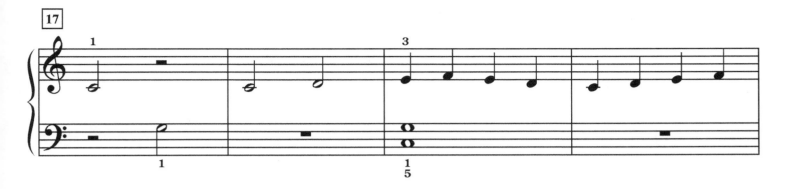

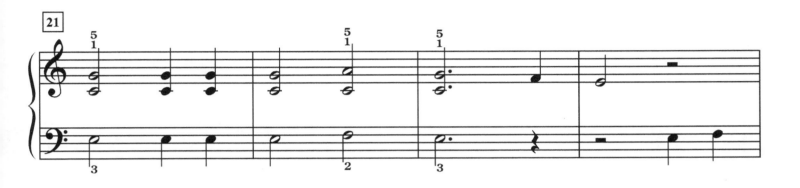

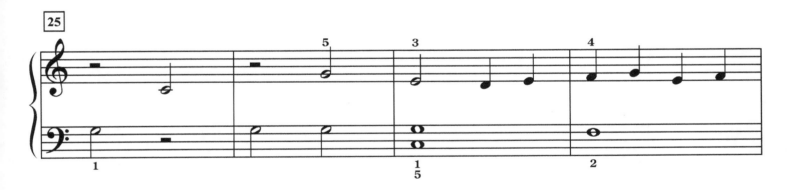

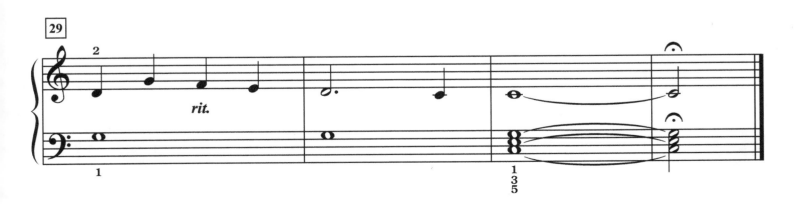

Egyptian Ballet Dance

(from the opera *Samson and Delilah*)

Camille Saint-Saëns (1835–1921)
Arranged by Carol Matz

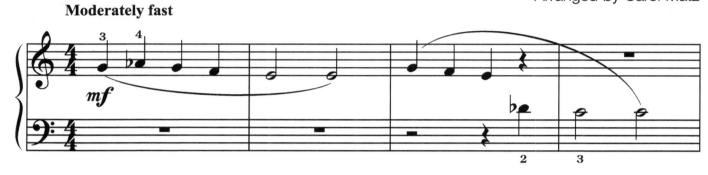

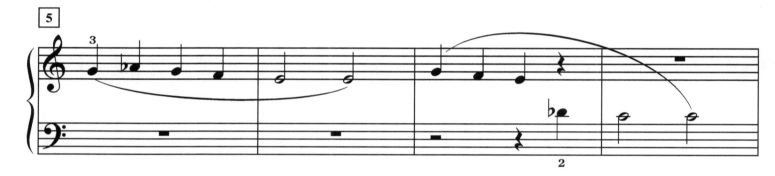

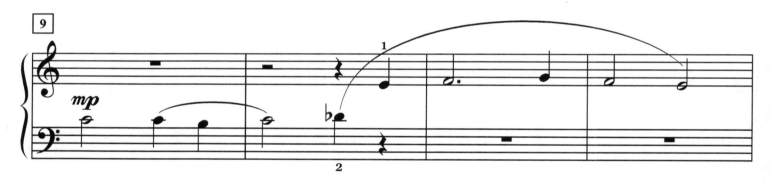

DUET PART (Student plays one octave higher)

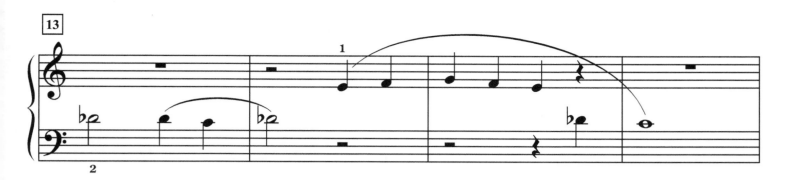

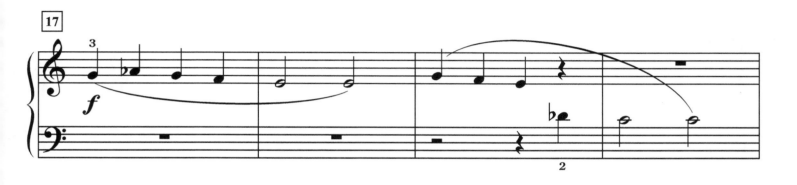

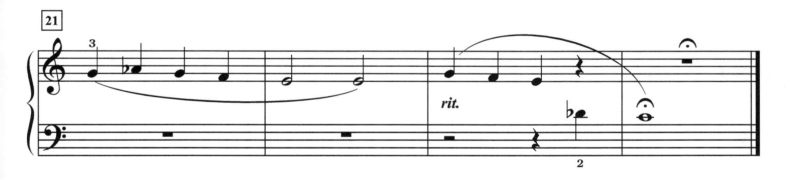

DUET PART (Continued)

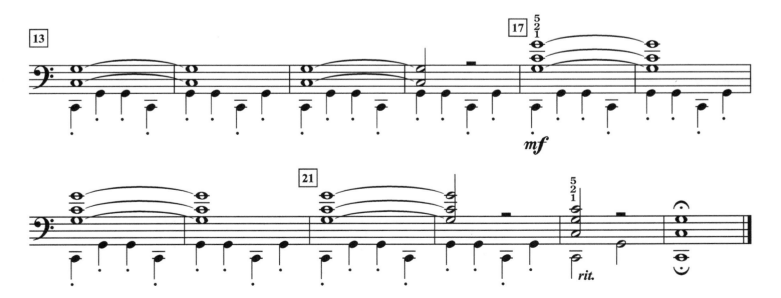

In the Hall of the Mountain King

(from *Peer Gynt Suite*)

Edvard Grieg (1843–1907)
Arranged by Carol Matz

DUET PART (Student plays as written)

DUET PART (Continued)

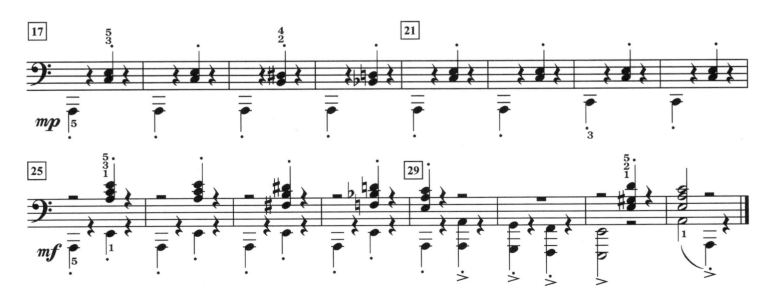

Auld Lang Syne

Traditional Scottish Melody
Words by Robert Burns
Arranged by Carol Matz

Expressively

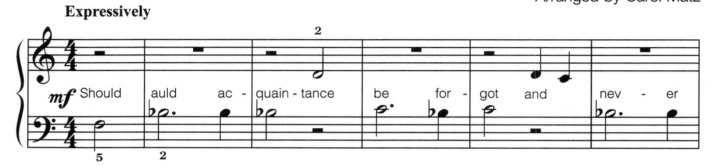

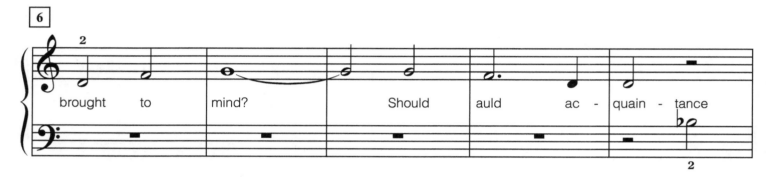

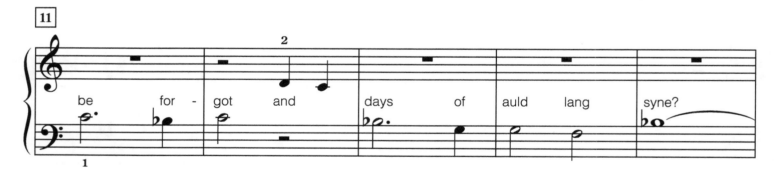

DUET PART (Student plays one octave higher)

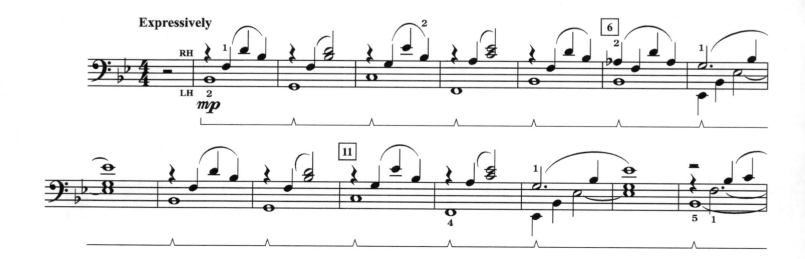

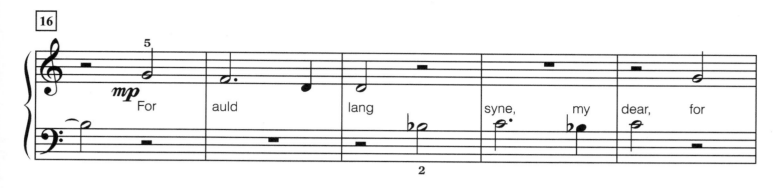

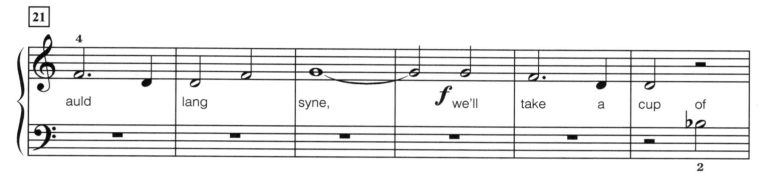

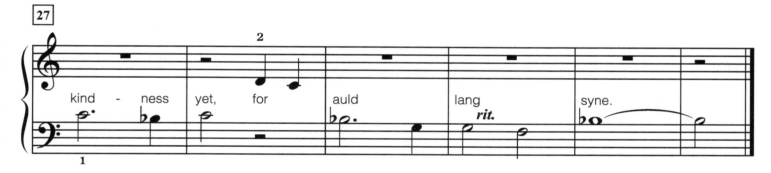

DUET PART (Continued)

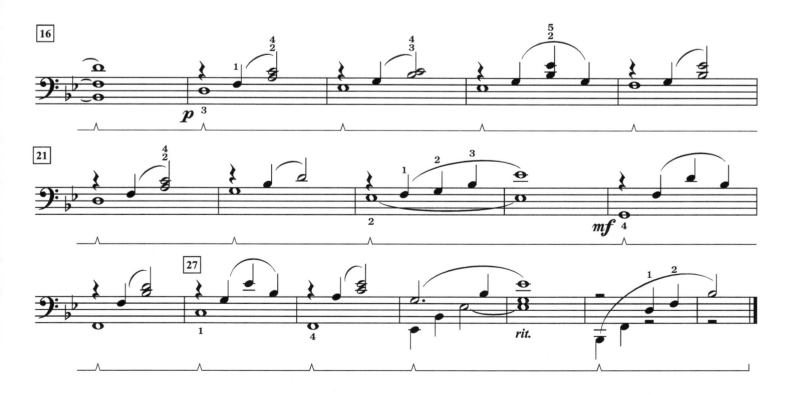

Take Me Out to the Ball Game

Words by Jack Norworth
Music by Albert Von Tilzer
Arranged by Carol Matz

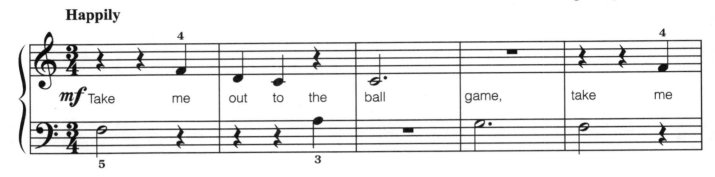

Take me out to the ball game, take me

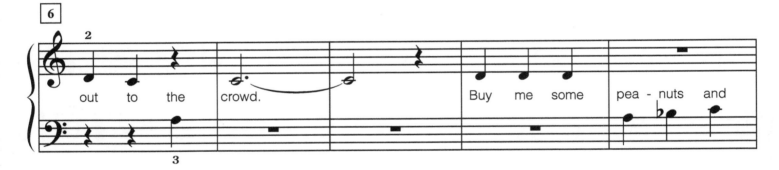

out to the crowd. Buy me some pea - nuts and

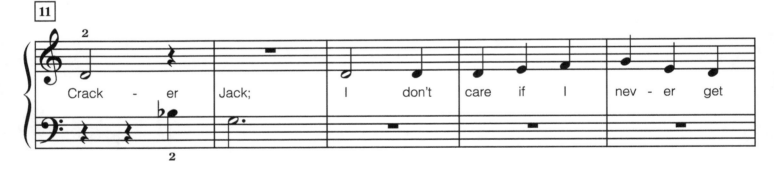

Crack - er Jack; I don't care if I nev - er get

DUET PART (Student plays one octave higher)

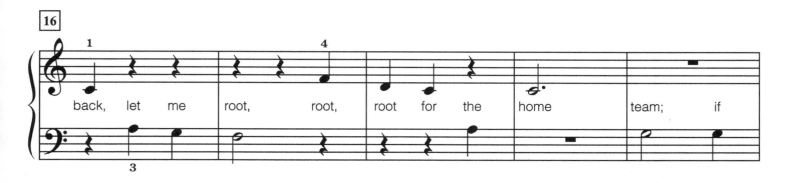

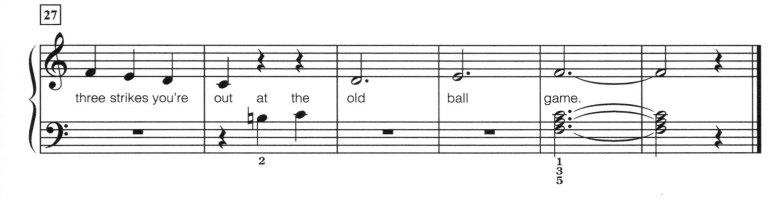

DUET PART (Continued)

The Ants Go Marching

Traditional
Arranged by Carol Matz

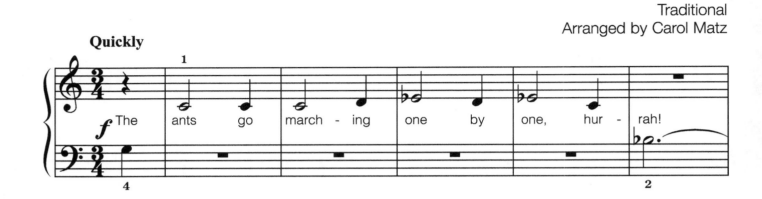

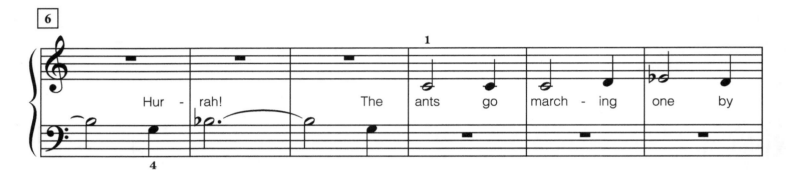

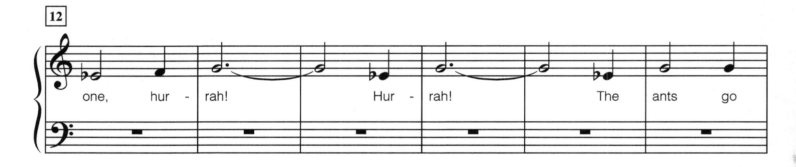

DUET PART (Student plays one octave higher)

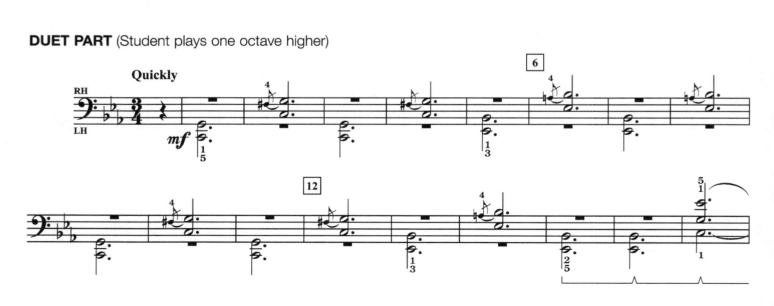

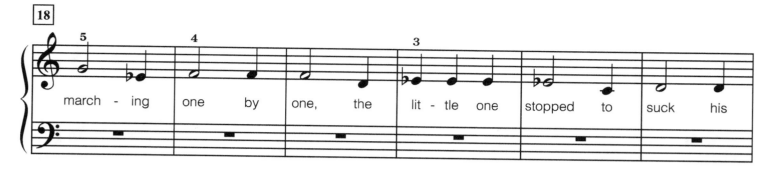

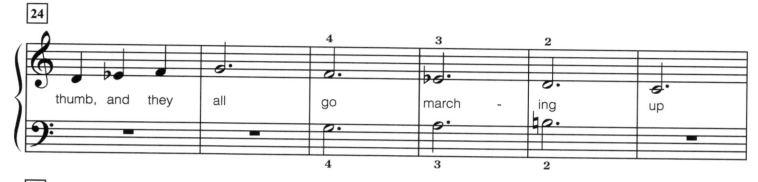

(Repeat for additional verses)

2. The ants go marching two by two . . .
   the little one stopped to tie his shoe . . . .

3. The ants go marching three by three . . .
   the little one stopped to climb a tree . . . .

4. The ants go marching four by four . . .
   the little one stopped to shut the door . . . .

5. The ants go marching five by five . . .
   the little one stopped to take a dive . . . .

6. The ants go marching six by six . . .
   the little one stopped to pick up sticks . . . .

7. The ants go marching seven by seven . . .
   the little one stopped to go to heaven . . . .

8. The ants go marching eight by eight . . .
   the little one stopped to shut the gate . . . .

9. The ants go marching nine by nine . . .
   the little one stopped and fell behind . . . .

10. The ants go marching ten by ten . . .
    the little one stopped to say "The End" . . . .

DUET PART (Continued)

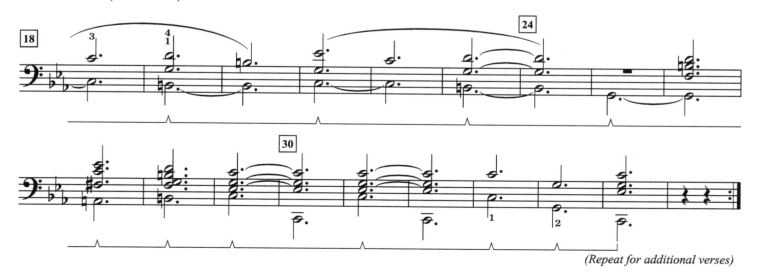

(Repeat for additional verses)

America the Beautiful

Words by Katherine Lee Bates
Music by Samuel A. Ward
Arranged by Carol Matz

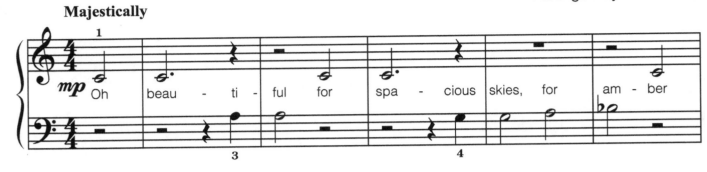

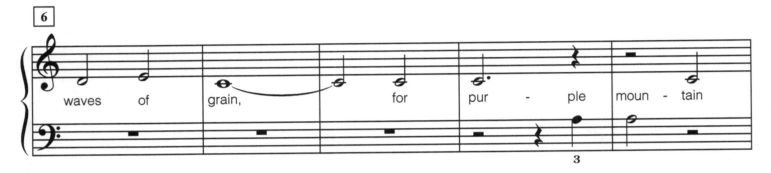

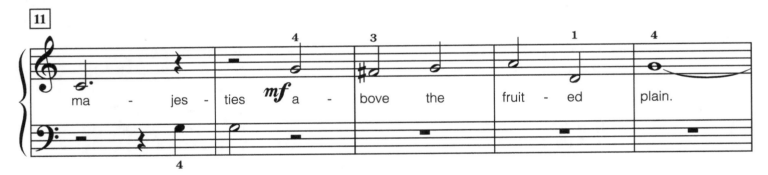

DUET PART (Student plays one octave higher)

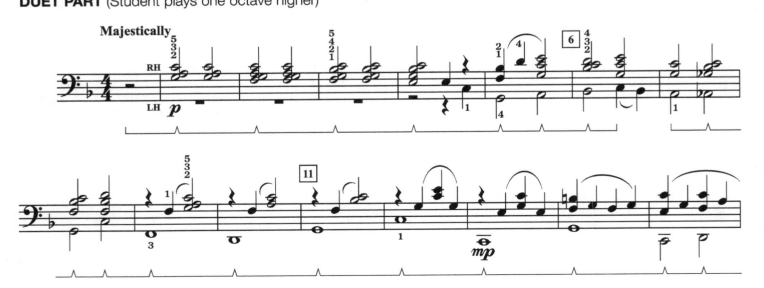

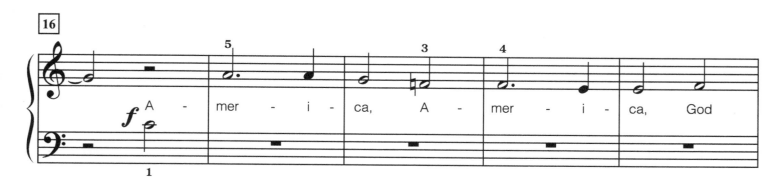

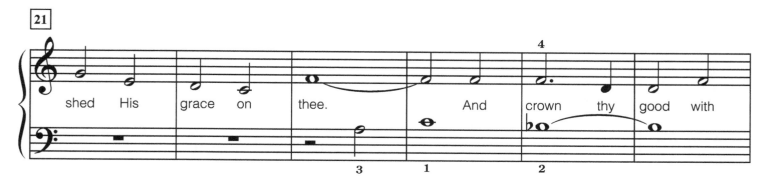

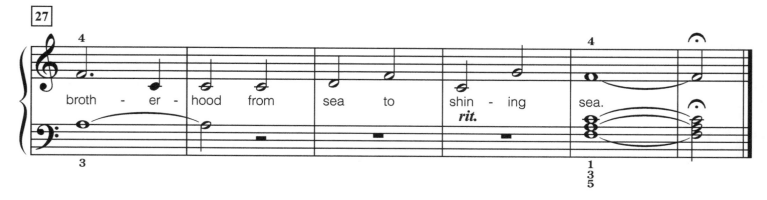

DUET PART (Continued)

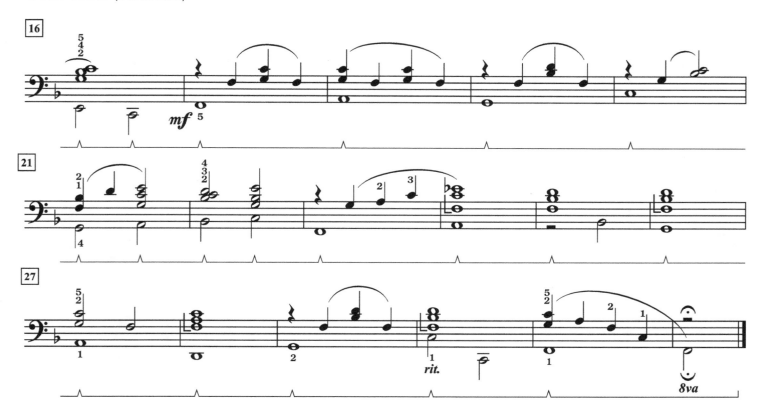

When the Saints Go Marching In

Traditional
Arranged by Carol Matz

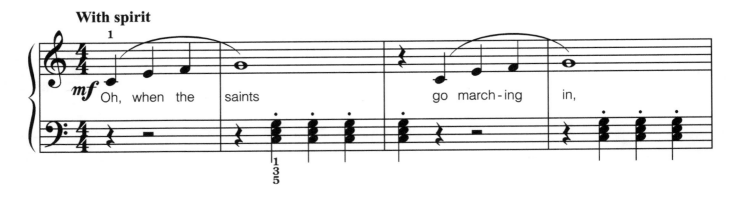

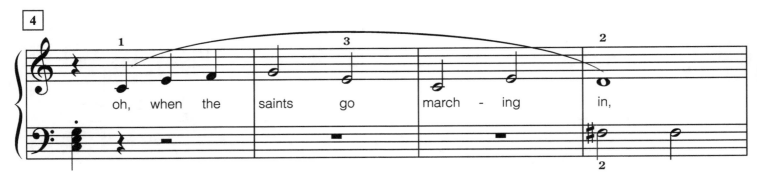

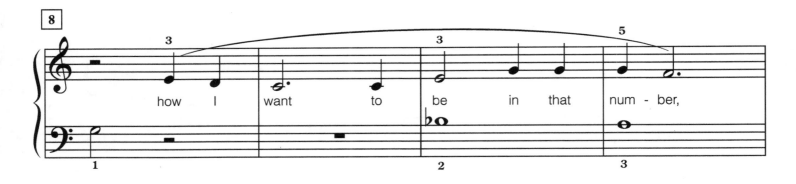

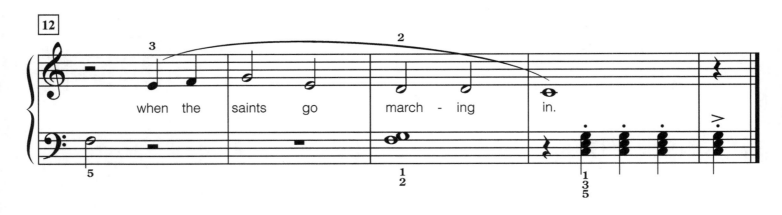

Boom, Boom!
(Ain't It Great to Be Crazy?)

Traditional
Arranged by Carol Matz

DUET PART (Student plays one octave higher)

Splish Splash

Words and Music by
Bobby Darin and Jean Murray
Arranged by Carol Matz

DUET PART (Student plays one octave higher)

DUET PART (Continued)

Boulevard of Broken Dreams

Lyrics by Billie Joe
Music by Green Day
Arranged by Carol Matz

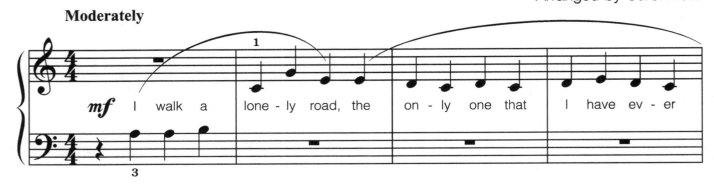

I walk a lone - ly road, the on - ly one that I have ev - er

known. Don't know where it goes, but it's home to me, I walk a - lone.

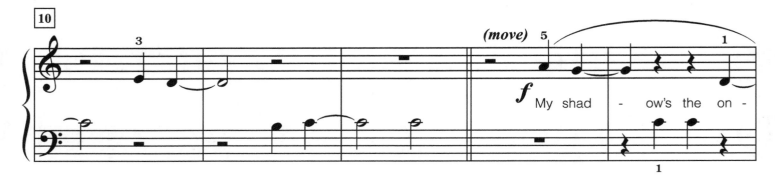

My shad - ow's the on -

DUET PART (Student plays one octave higher)

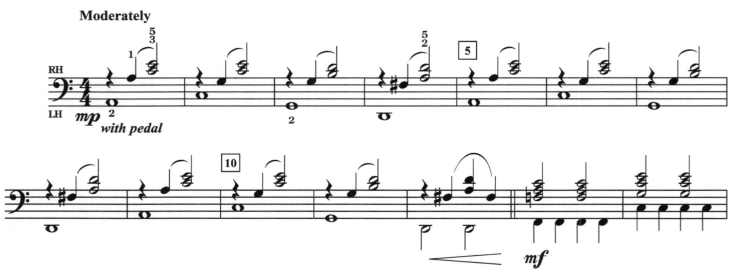

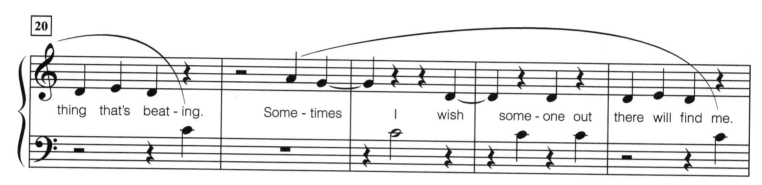

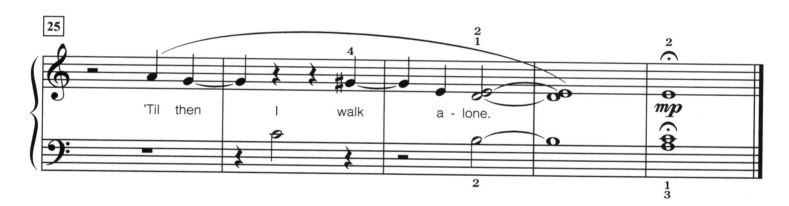

DUET PART (Continued)

Hey There Delilah

Words and Music by Tom Higgenson
Arranged by Carol Matz

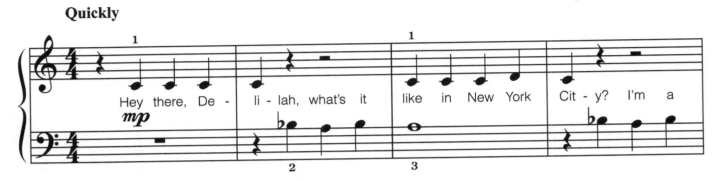

DUET PART (Student plays one octave higher)

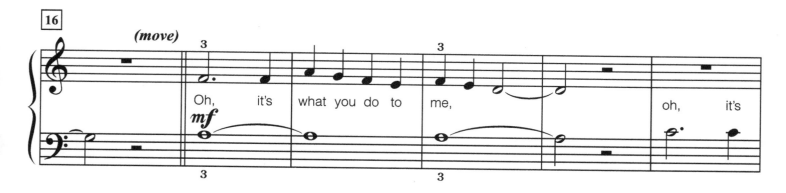

Oh, it's what you do to me, oh, it's

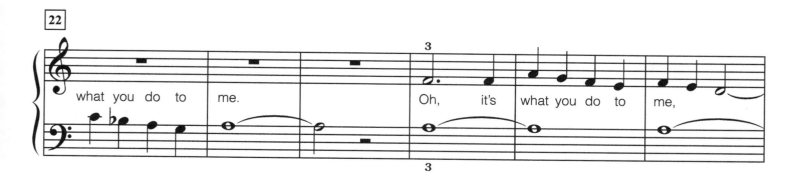

what you do to me. Oh, it's what you do to me,

oh, it's what you do to me, what you do to me.

DUET PART (Continued)

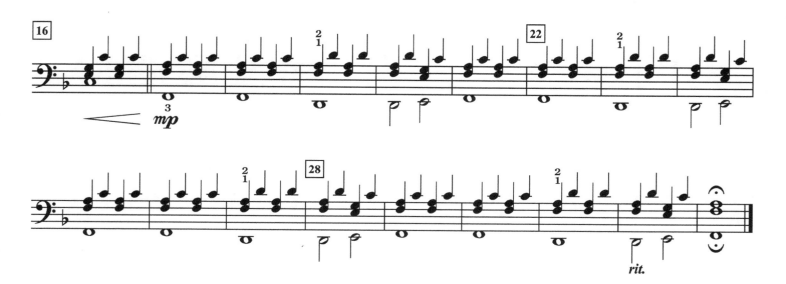

All I Have to Do Is Dream

Words and Music by Boudleaux Bryant
Arranged by Carol Matz

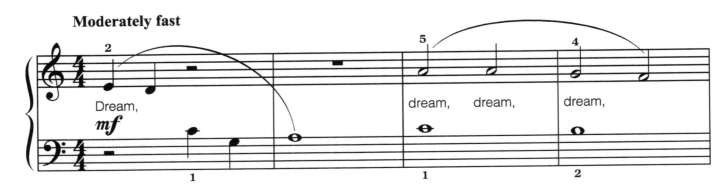

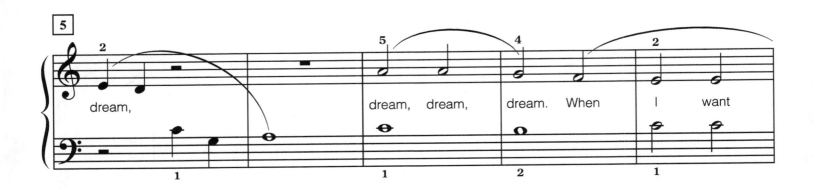

DUET PART (Student plays one octave higher)

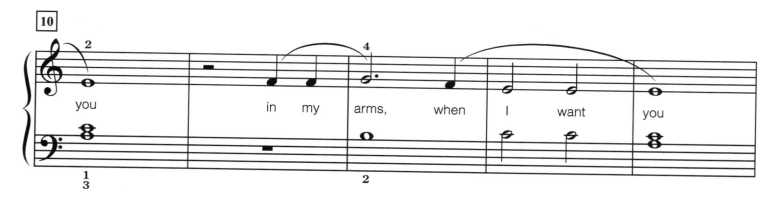

you in my arms, when I want you

and all your charms, when - ev - er I want you, all I have to

do is dream.

DUET PART (Continued)

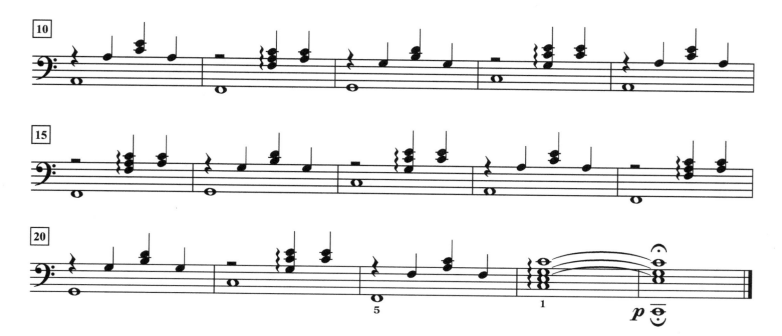

41

Eye of the Tiger

Words and Music by
Frankie Sullivan III and Jim Peterik
Arranged by Carol Matz

DUET PART (Student plays one octave higher)

Maple Leaf Rag

Secondo

Scott Joplin
Arranged by Carol Matz

Moderately fast

Play both hands one octave lower

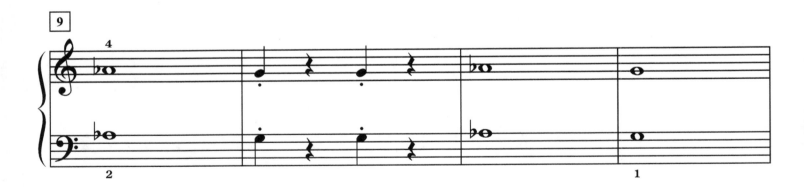

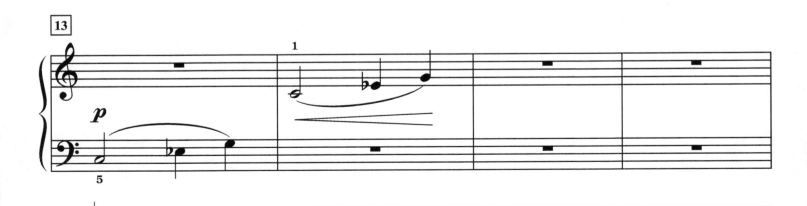

Maple Leaf Rag

Primo

Scott Joplin
Arranged by Carol Matz

Moderately fast
Play both hands one octave higher

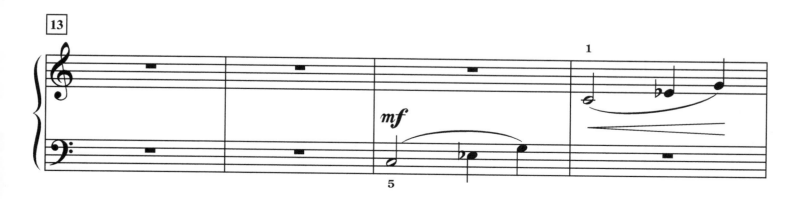

Secondo

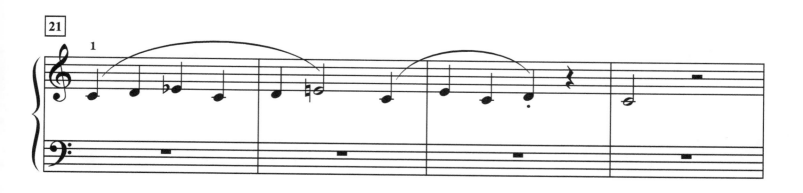

The Siamese Cat Song

(from Walt Disney's "The Lady and the Tramp")

Secondo

Words and Music by
Peggy Lee and Sonny Burke
Arranged by Carol Matz

The Siamese Cat Song

(from Walt Disney's "The Lady and the Tramp")

Primo

Words and Music by
Peggy Lee and Sonny Burke
Arranged by Carol Matz

Secondo

Do you see that thing swim-ming 'round and 'round?

May - be we could reach in and make it drown.

Wipe Out

Secondo

By The Surfaris
Arranged by Carol Matz

Quickly
Play both hands one octave lower

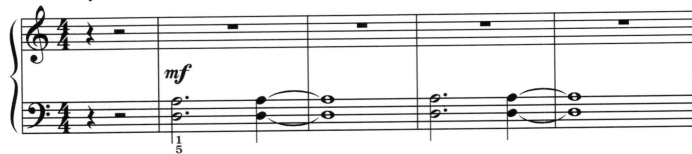

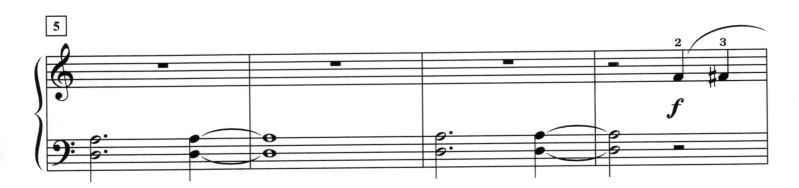

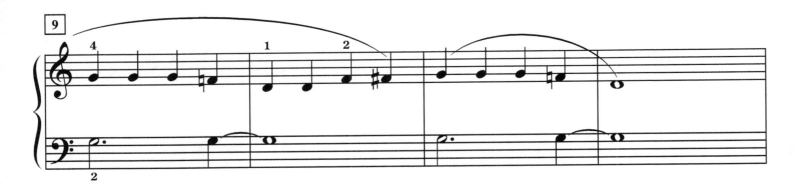

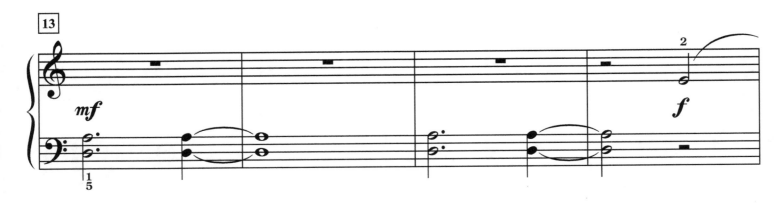

Wipe Out

Primo

By The Surfaris
Arranged by Carol Matz

Quickly
Play both hands one octave higher

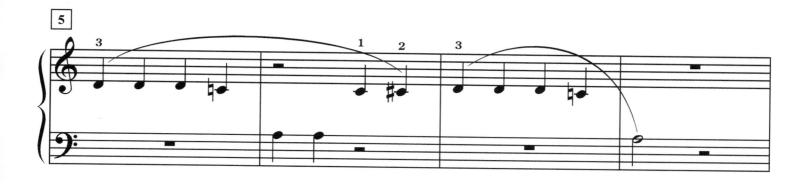

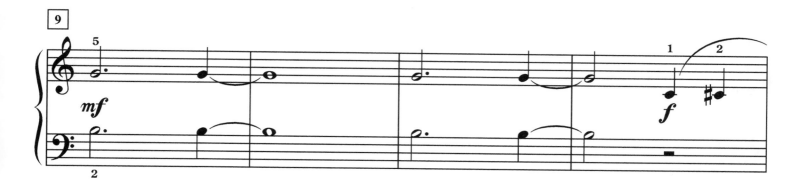

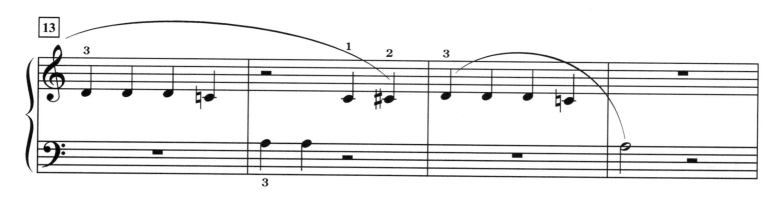

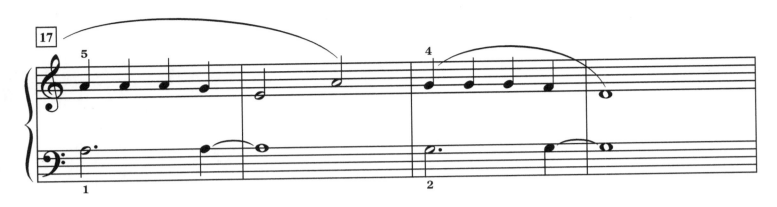

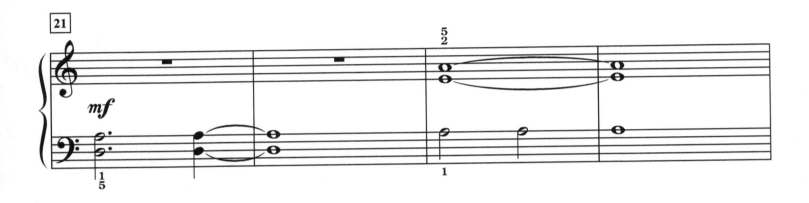

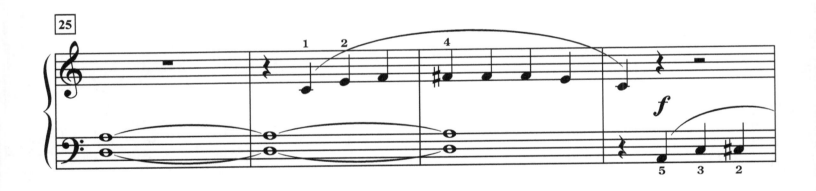

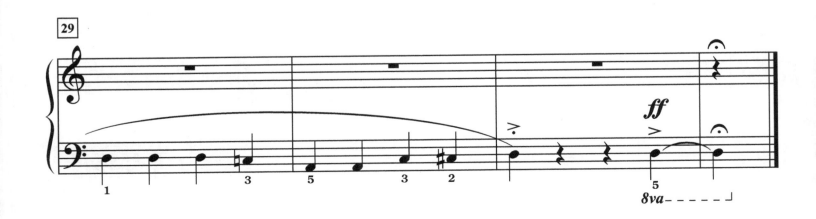

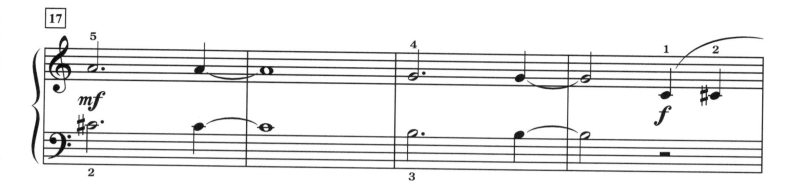

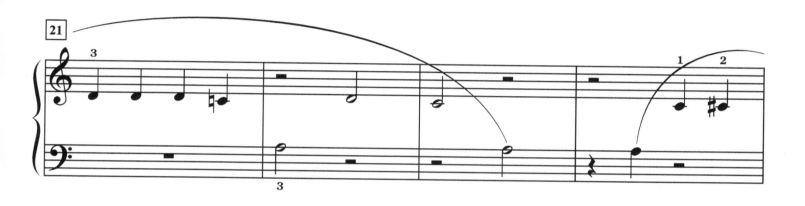

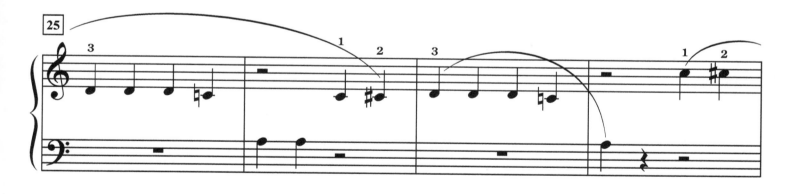

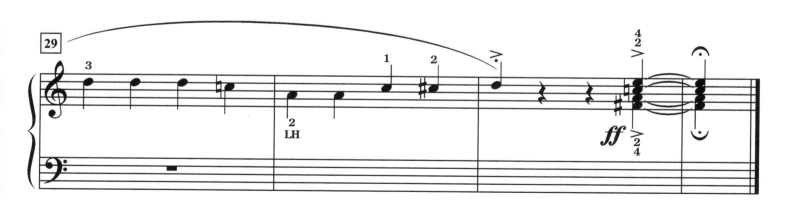